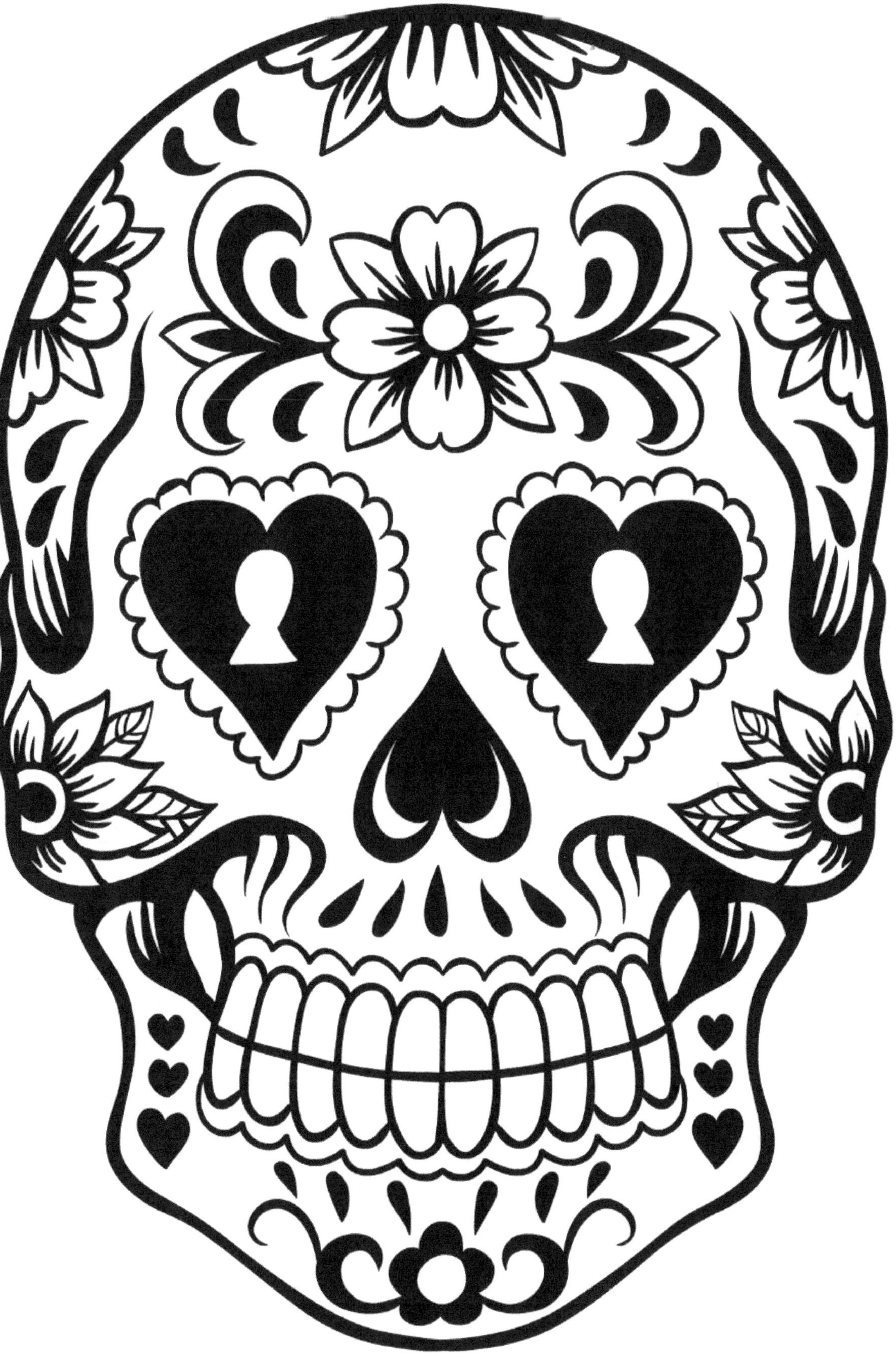

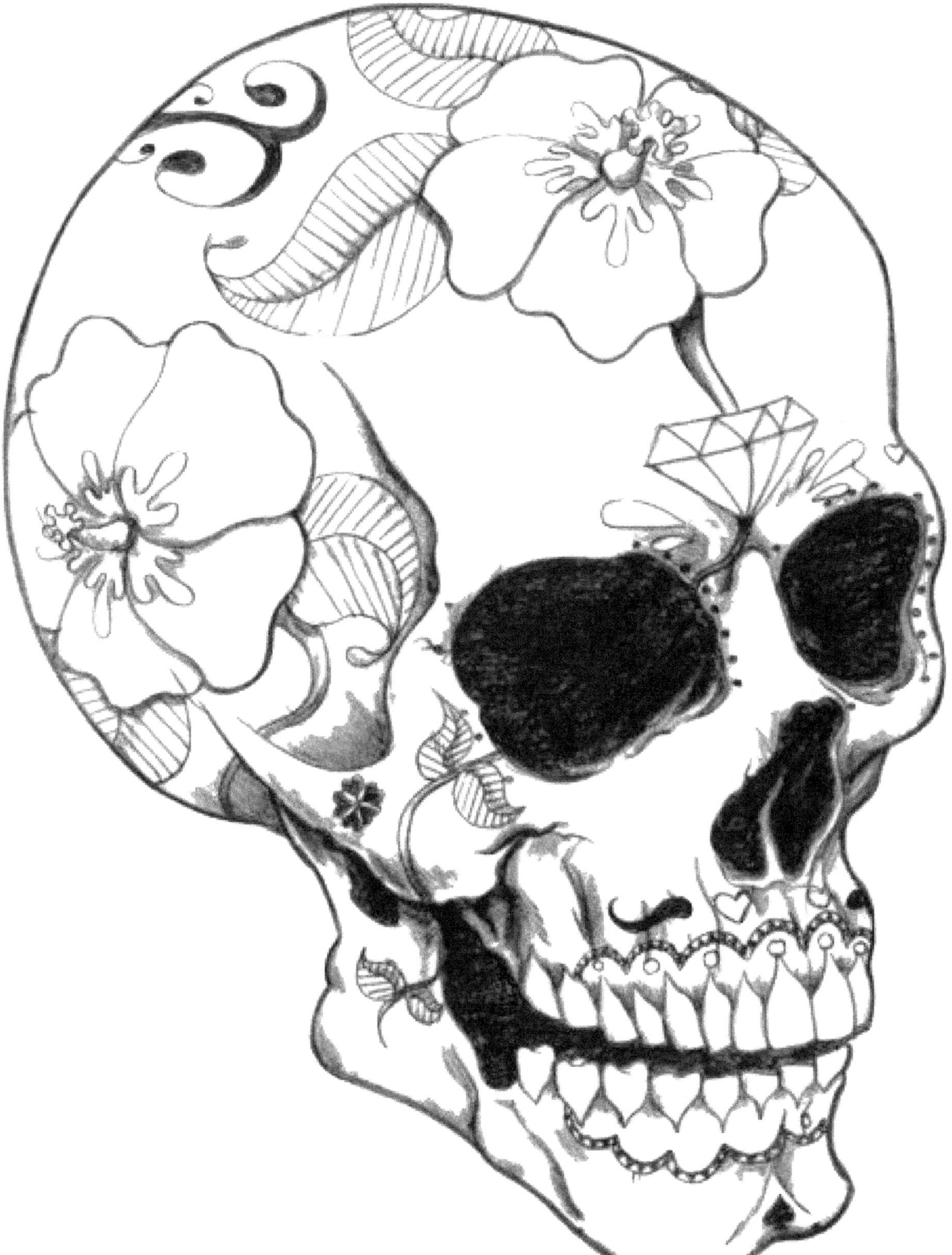

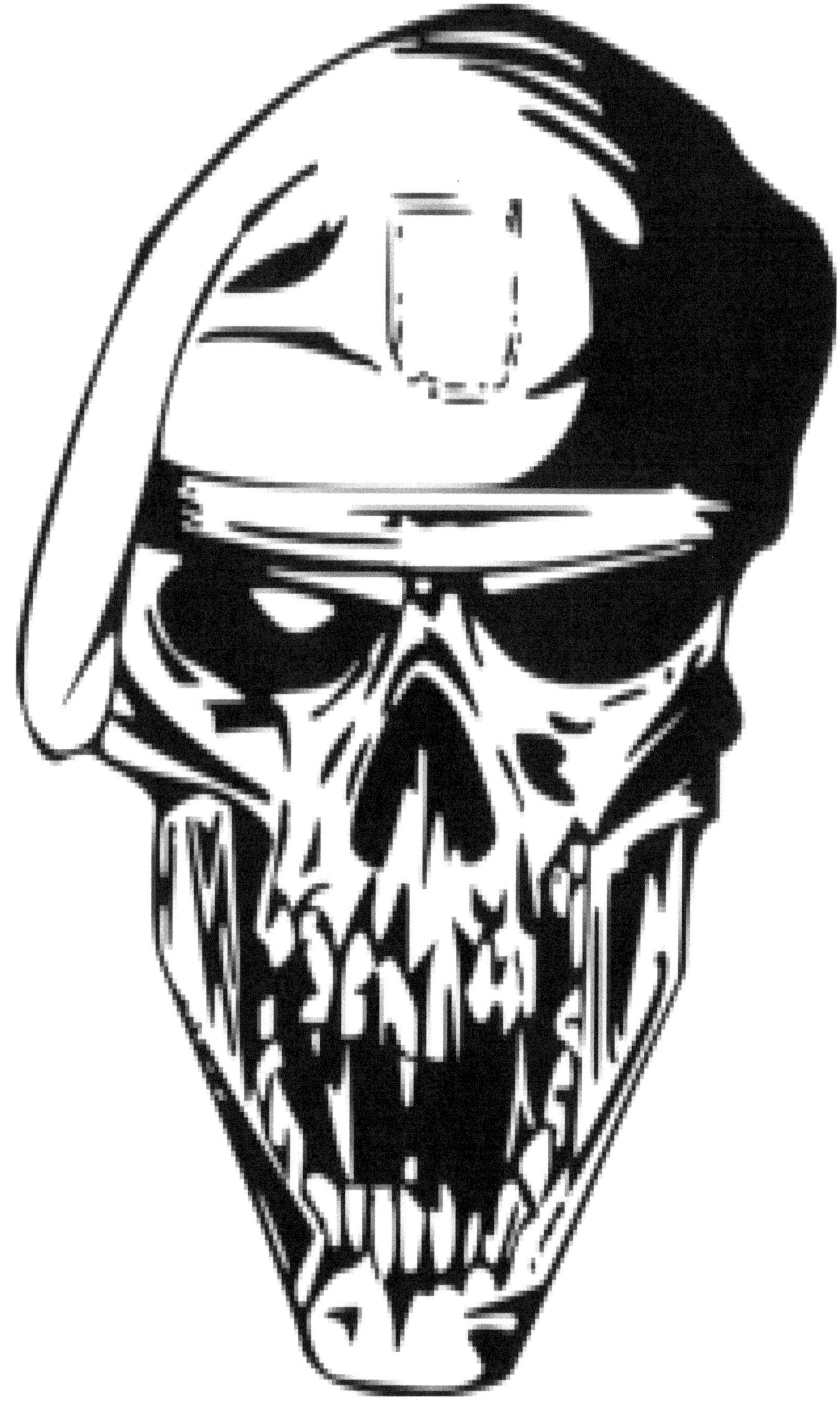

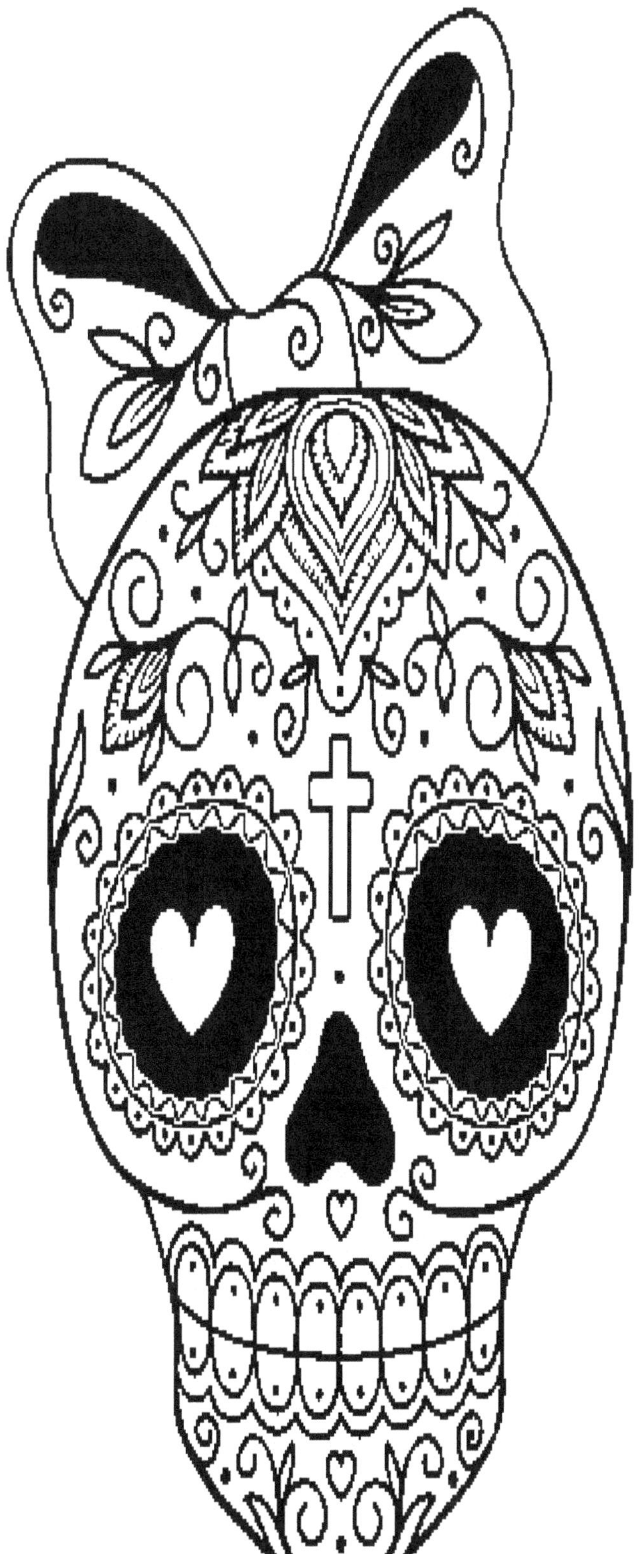

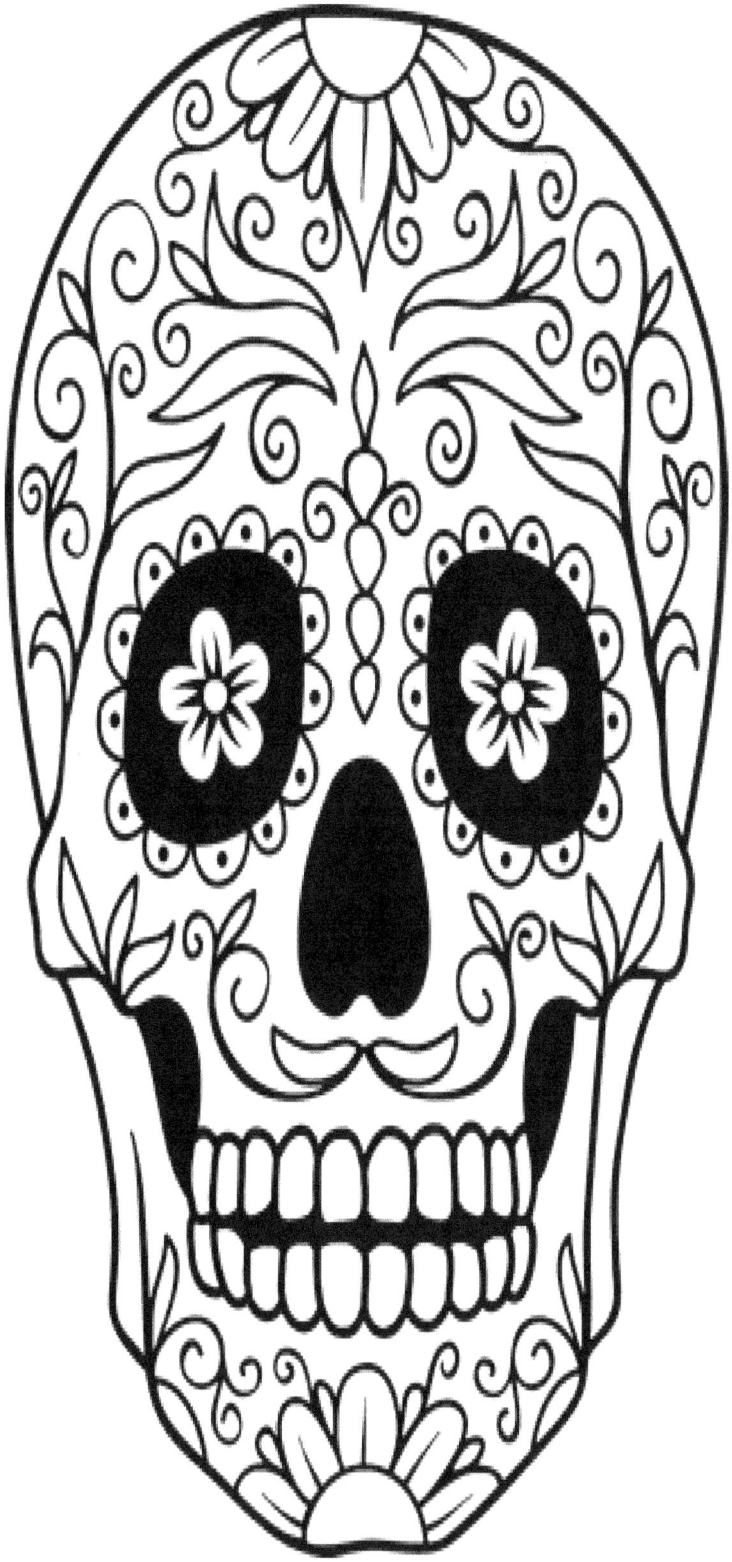

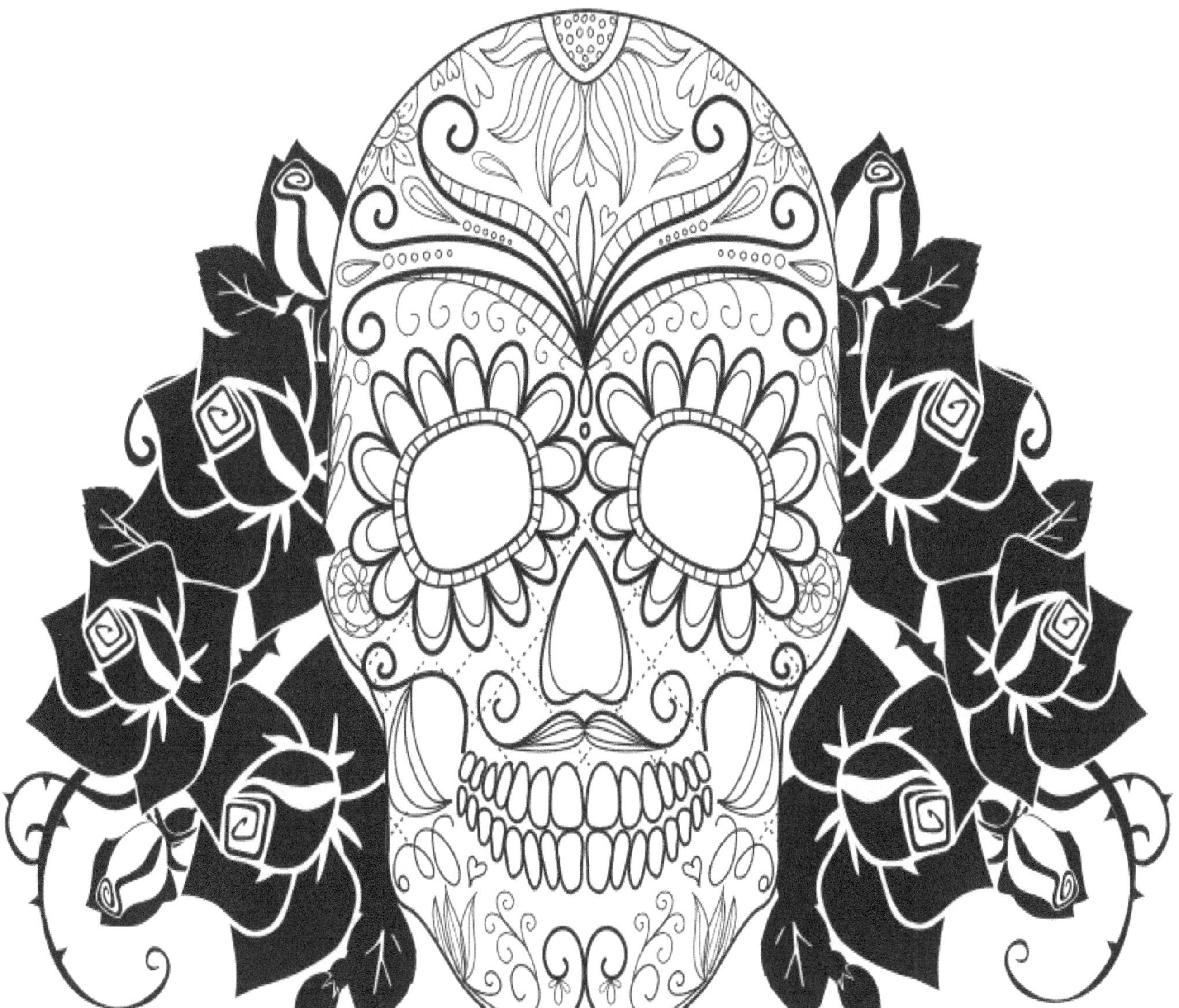

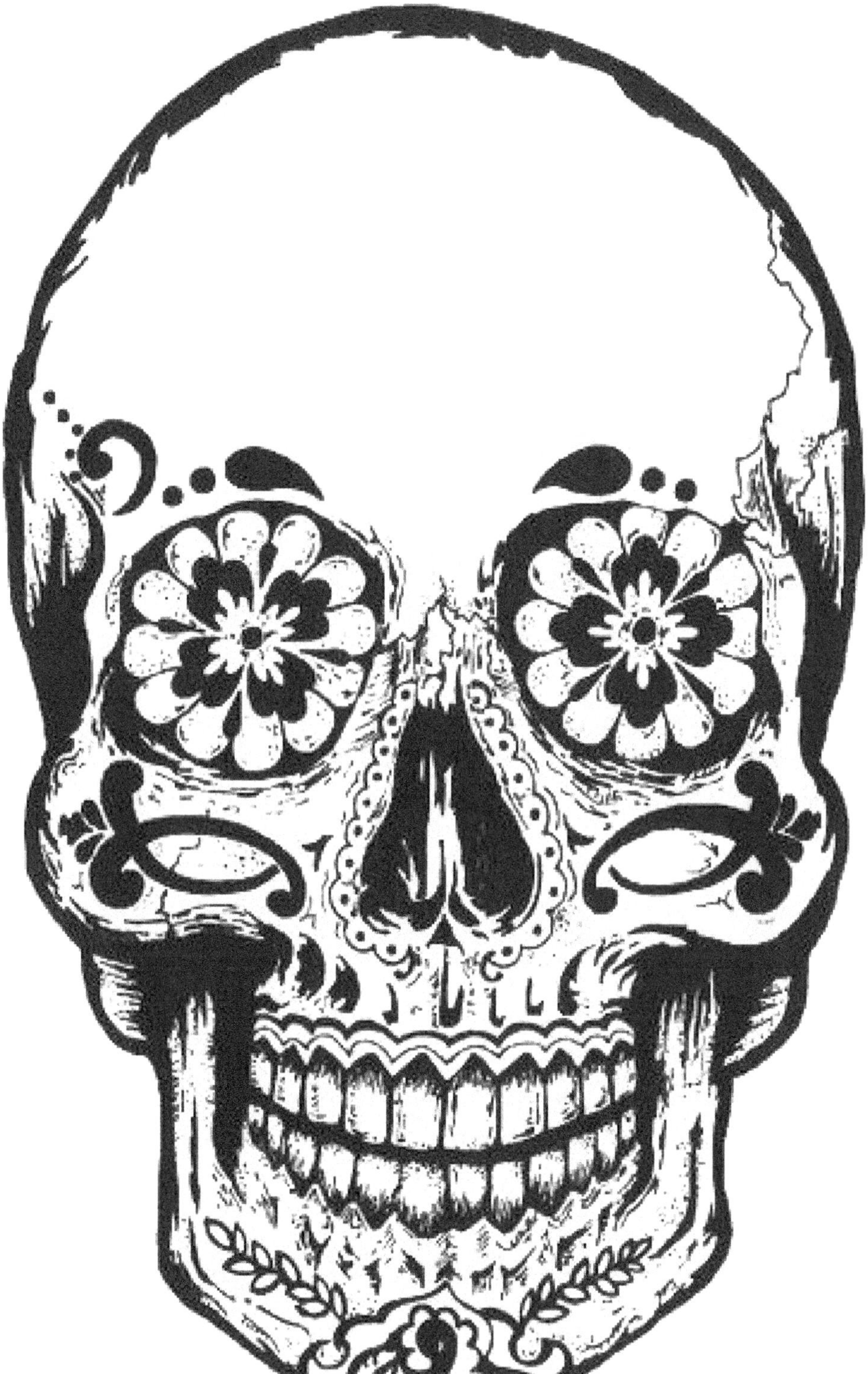

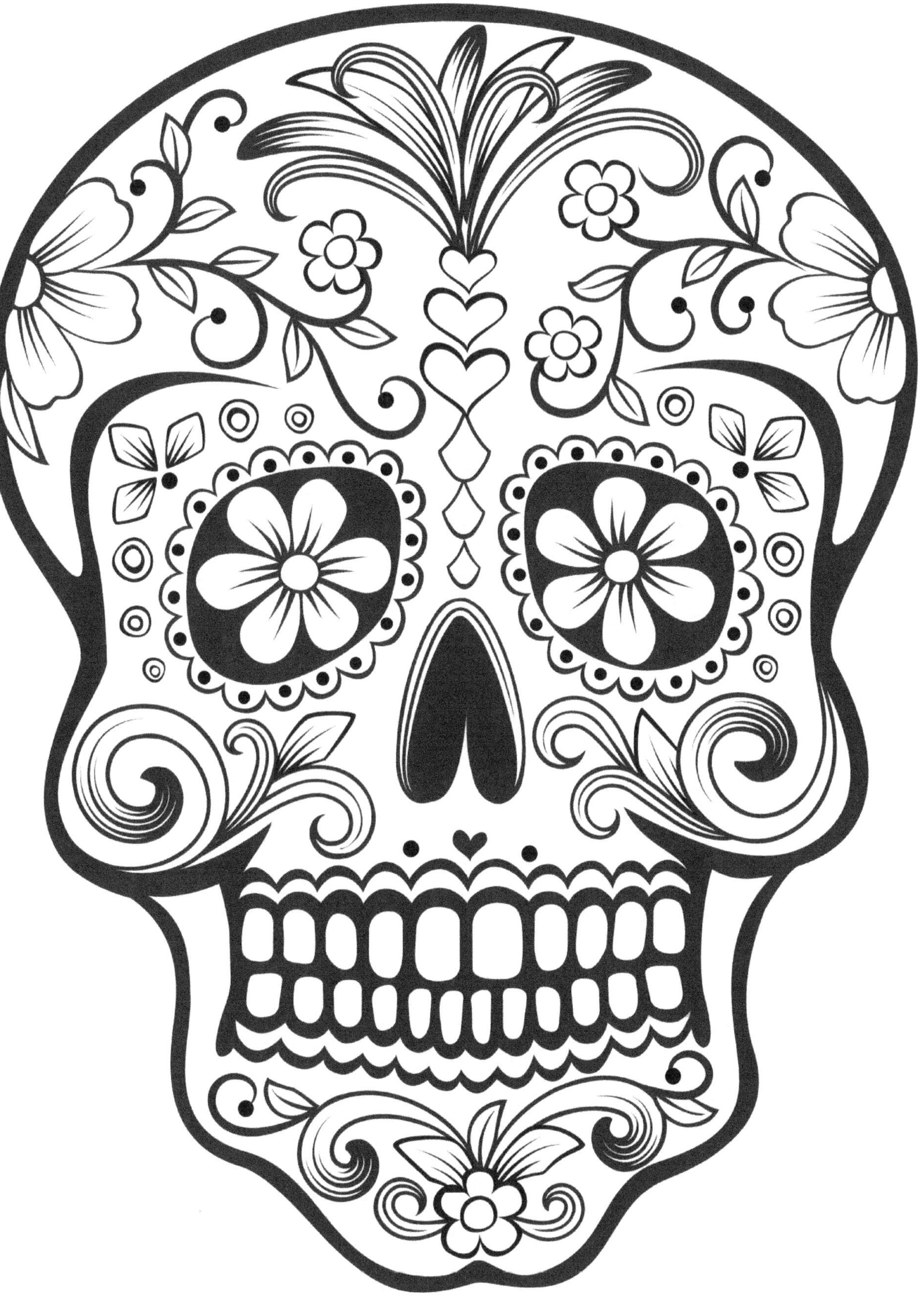

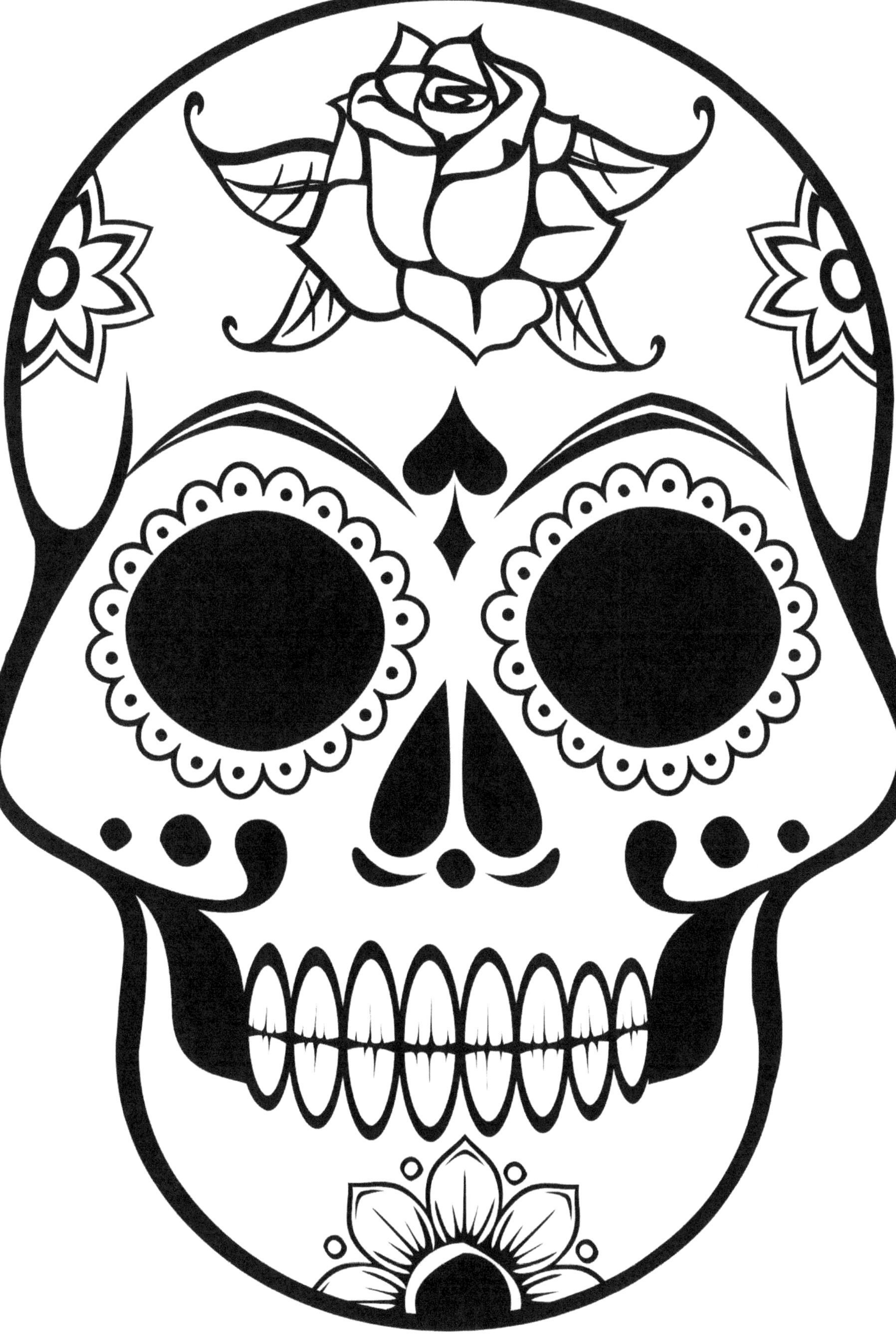

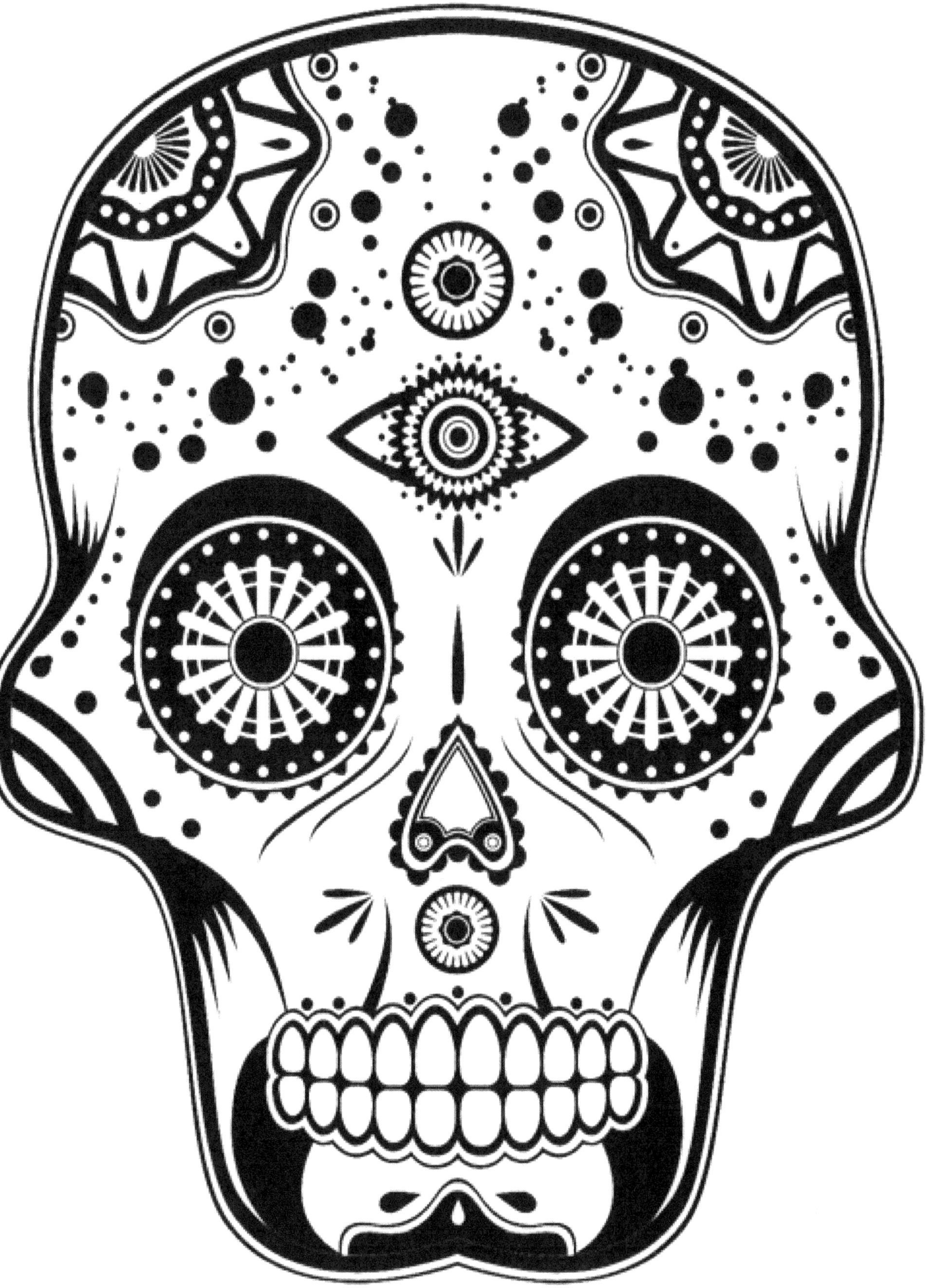

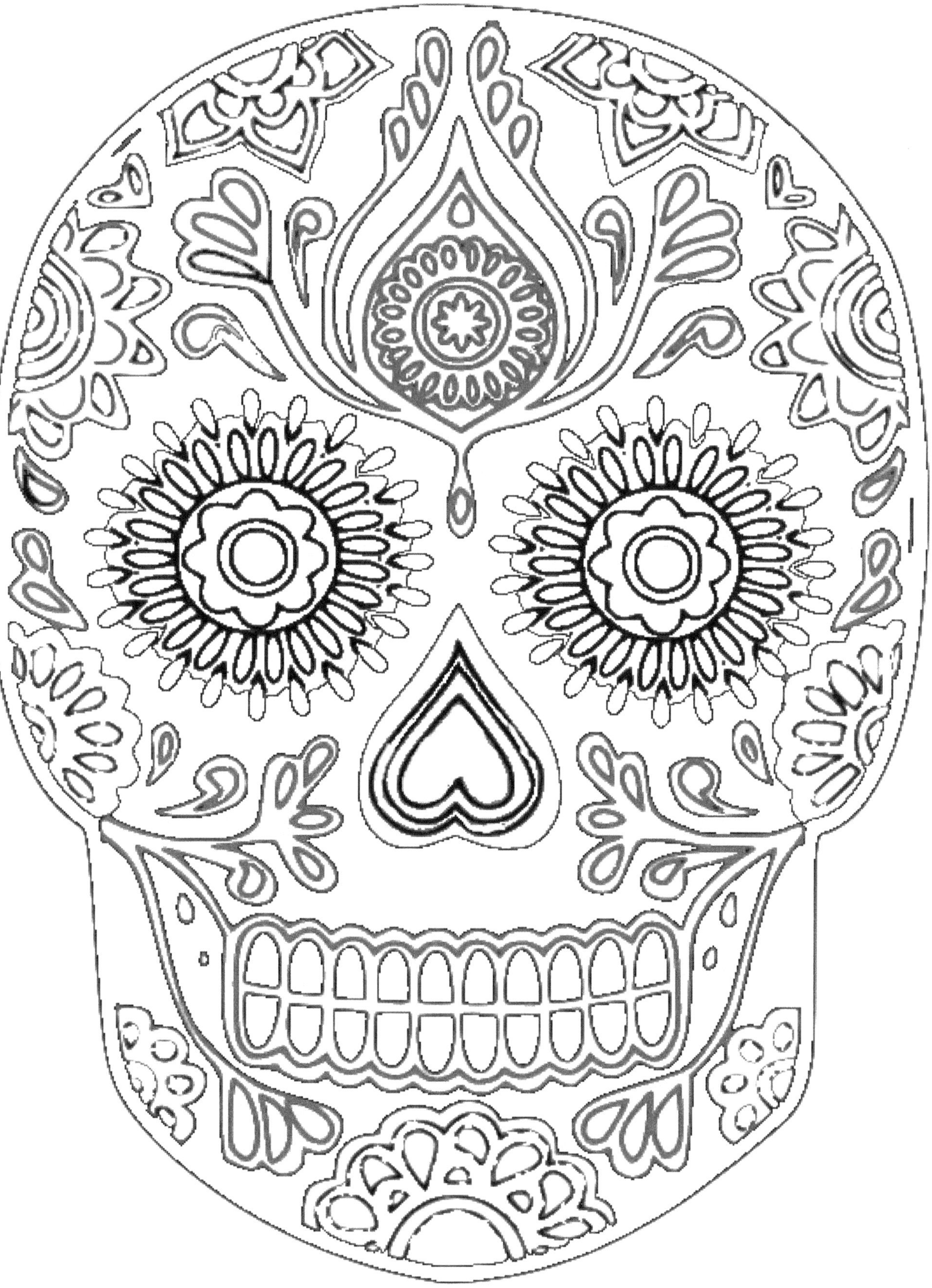

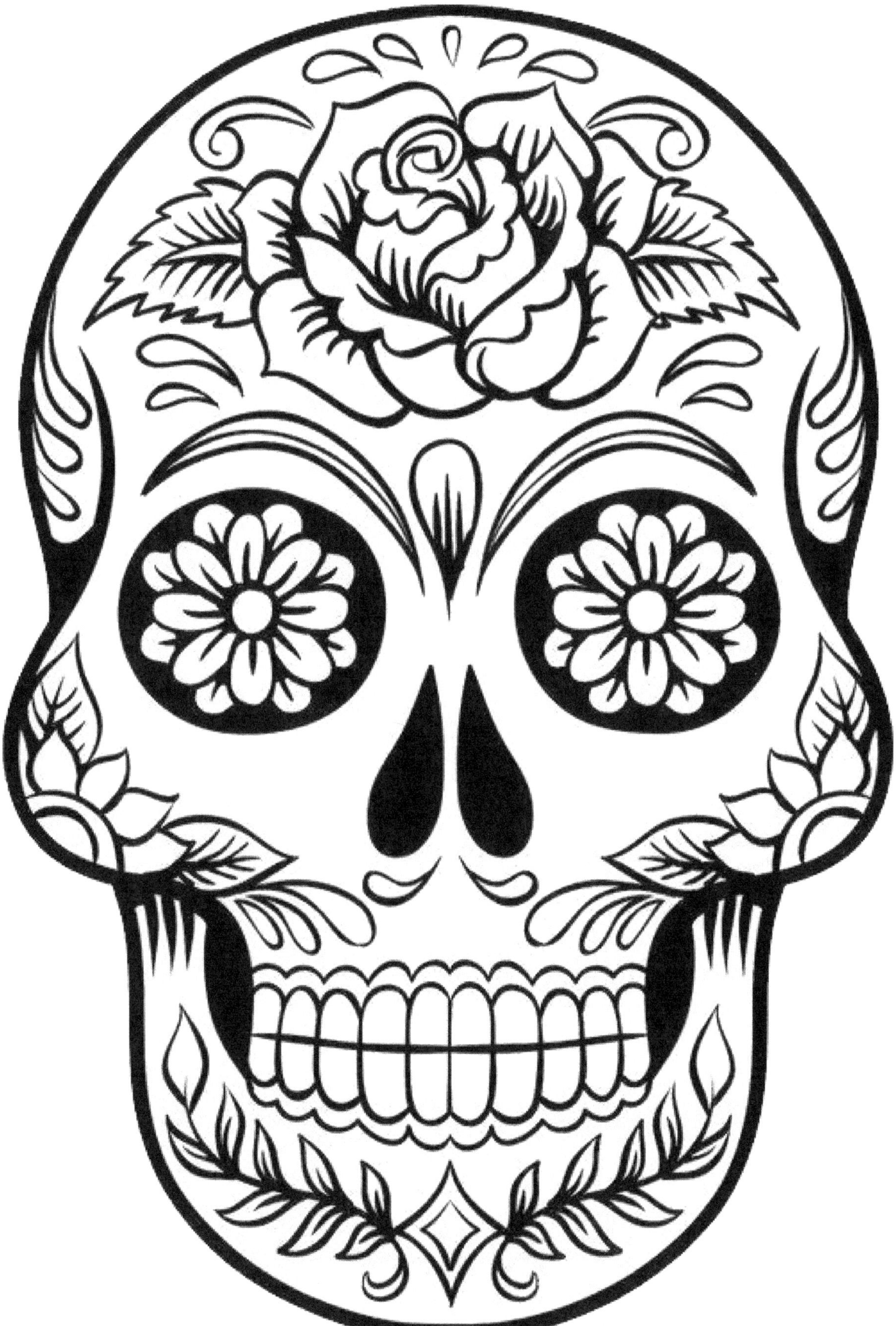

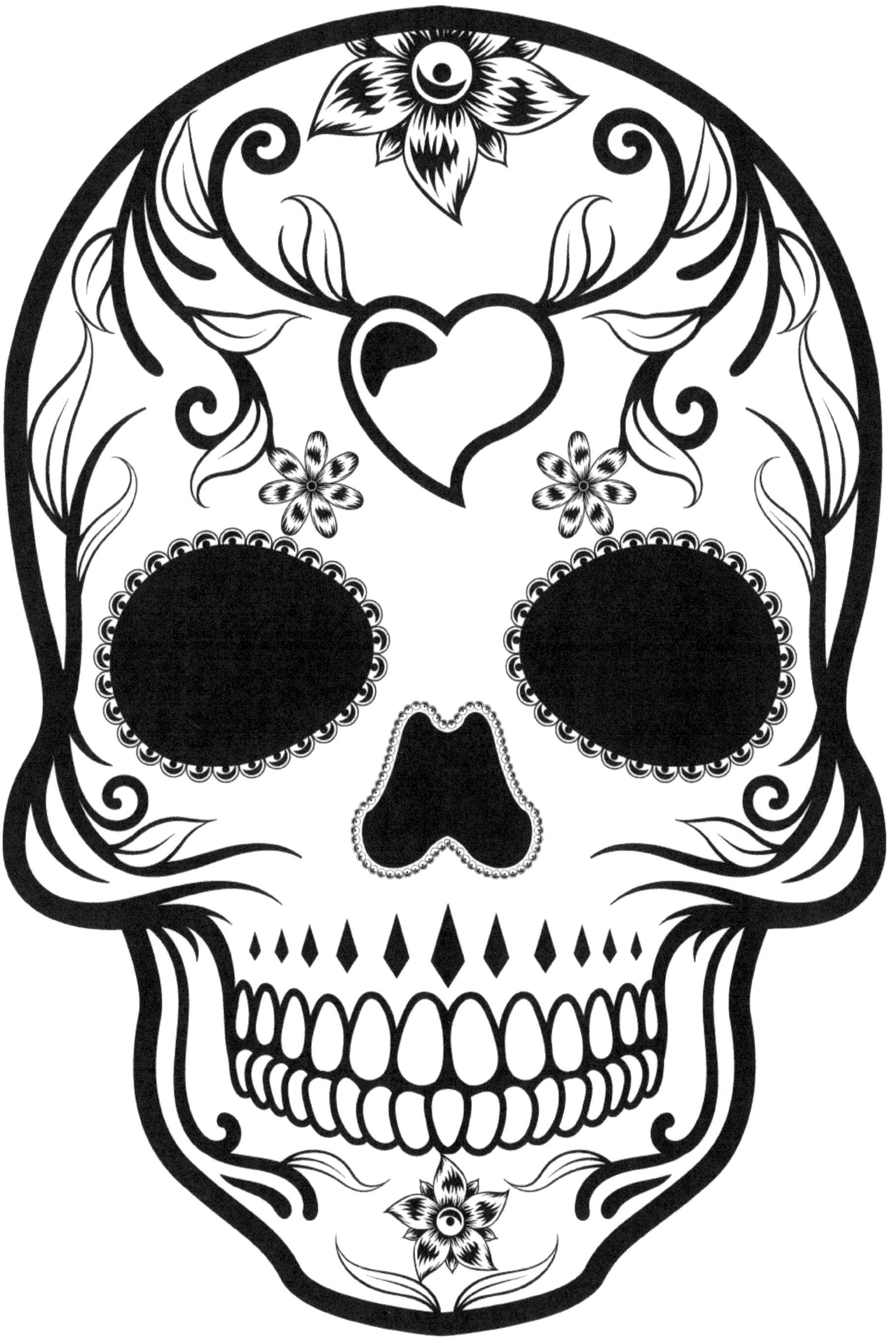

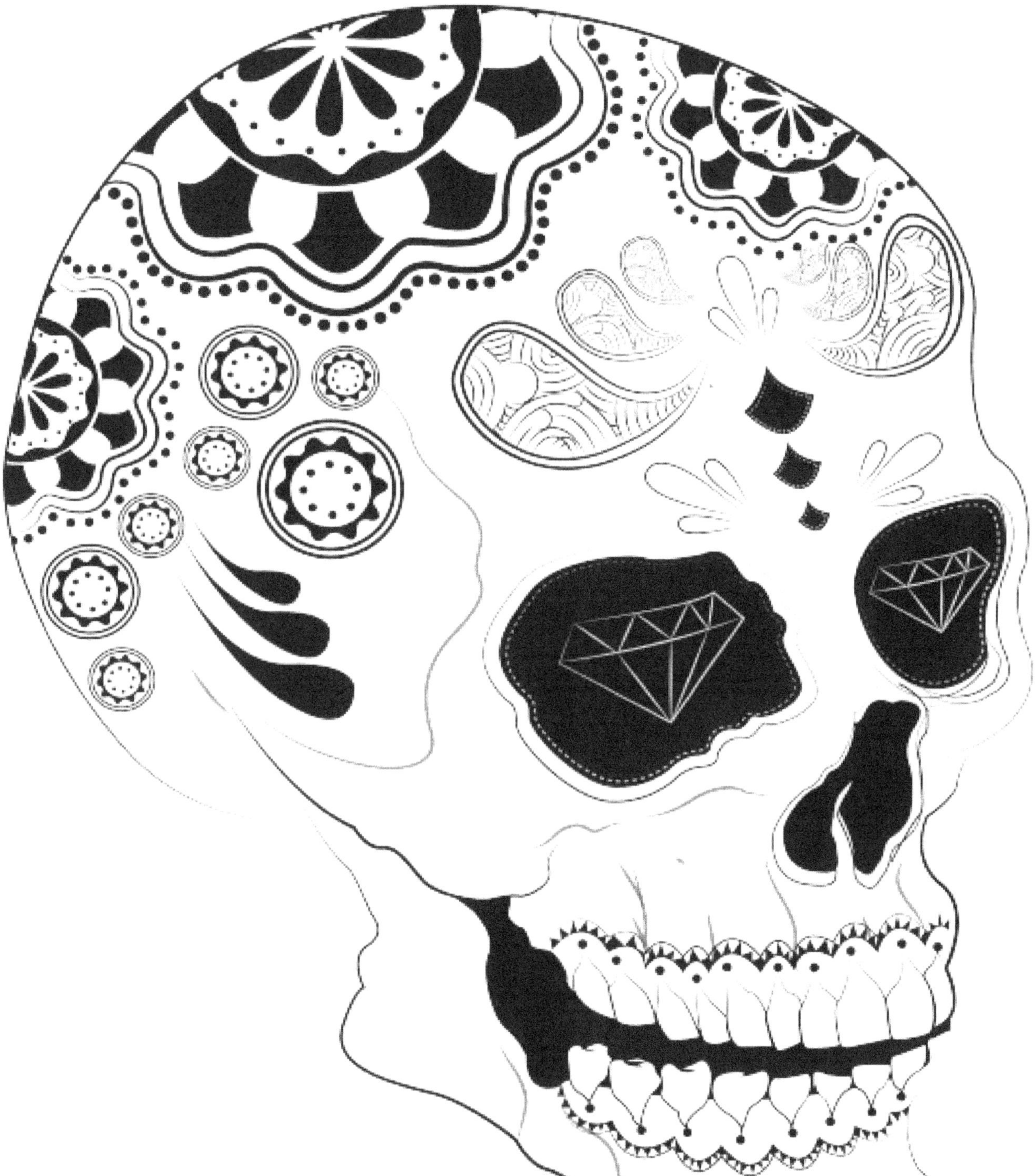

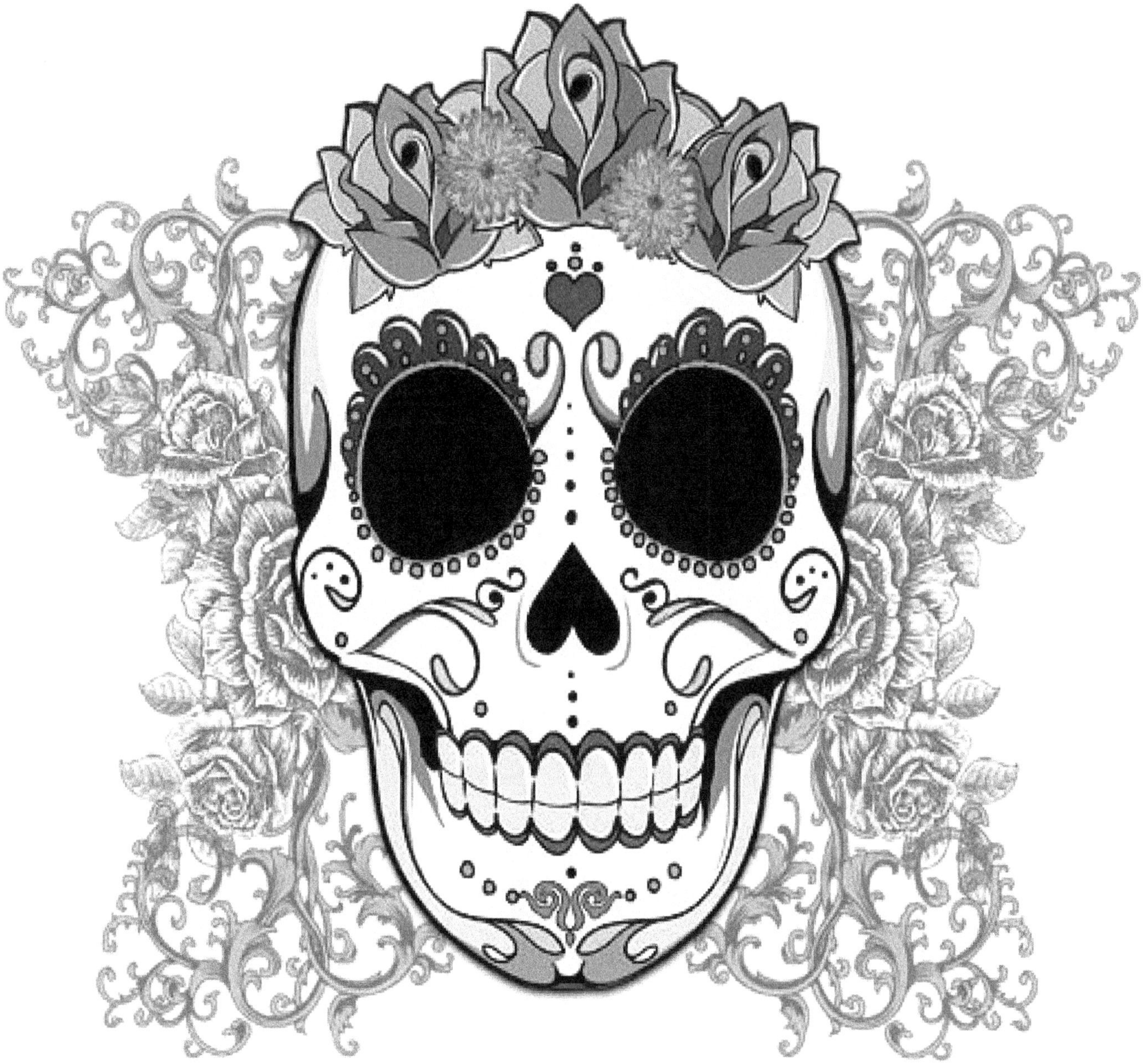

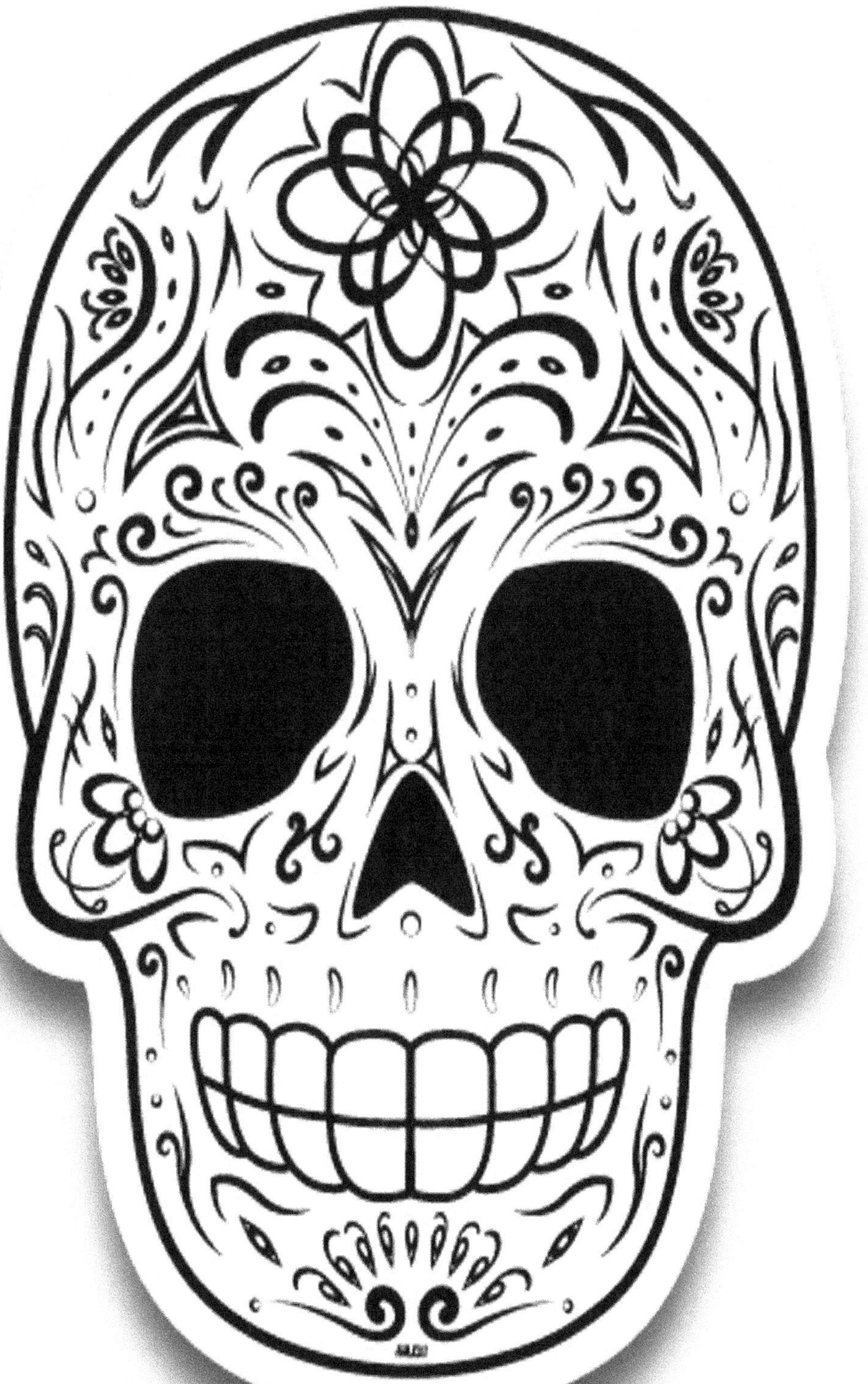

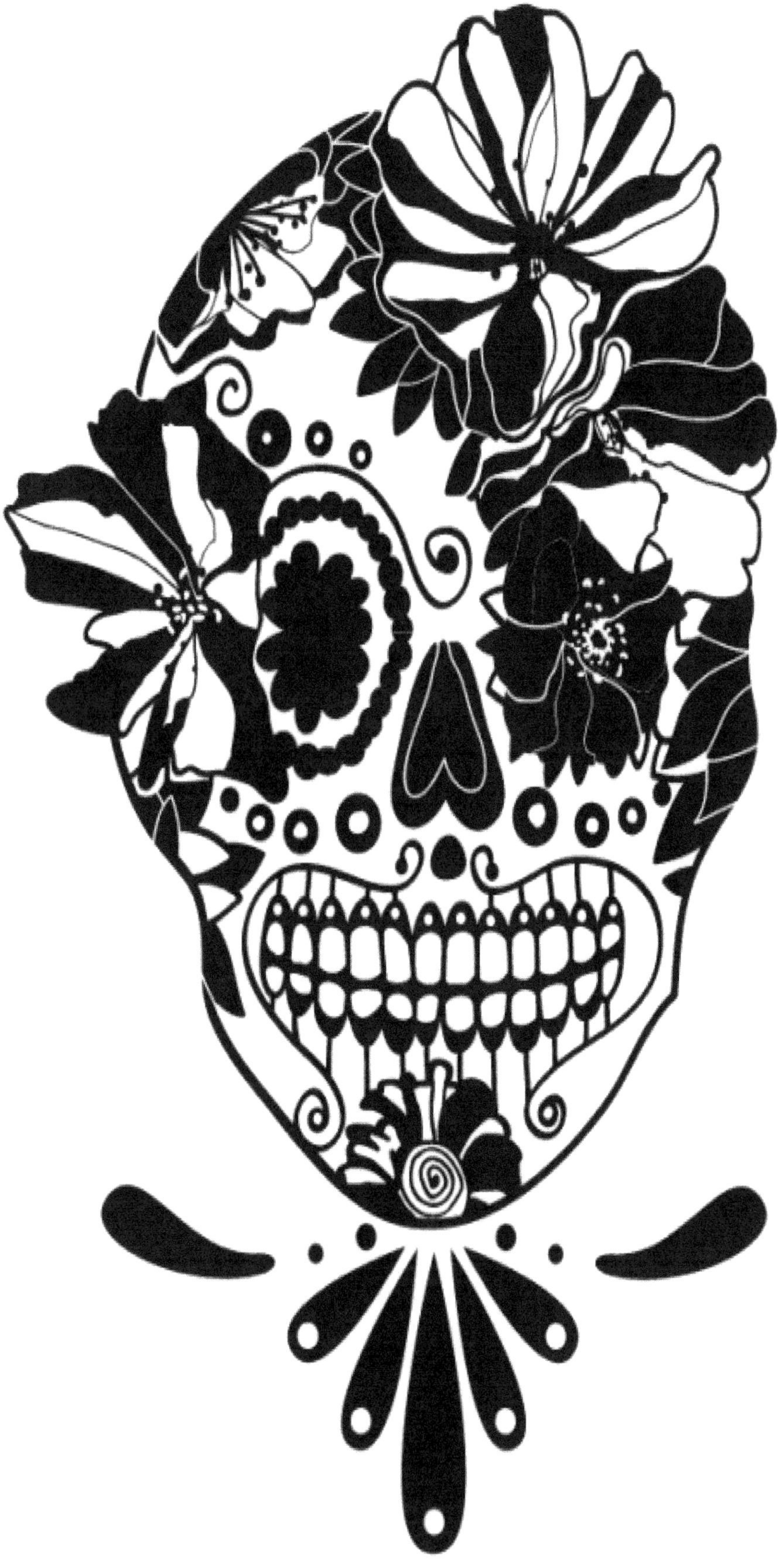

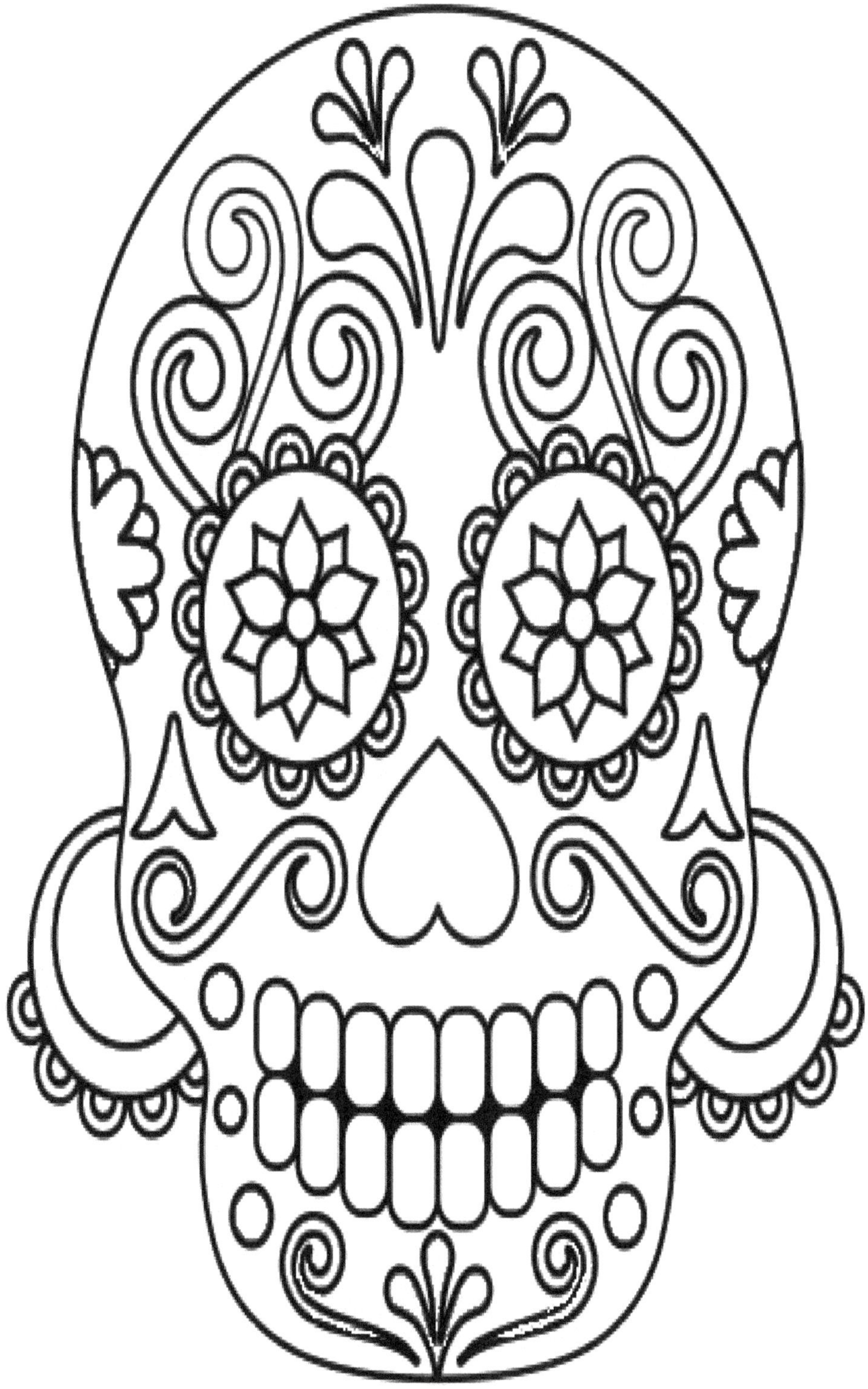

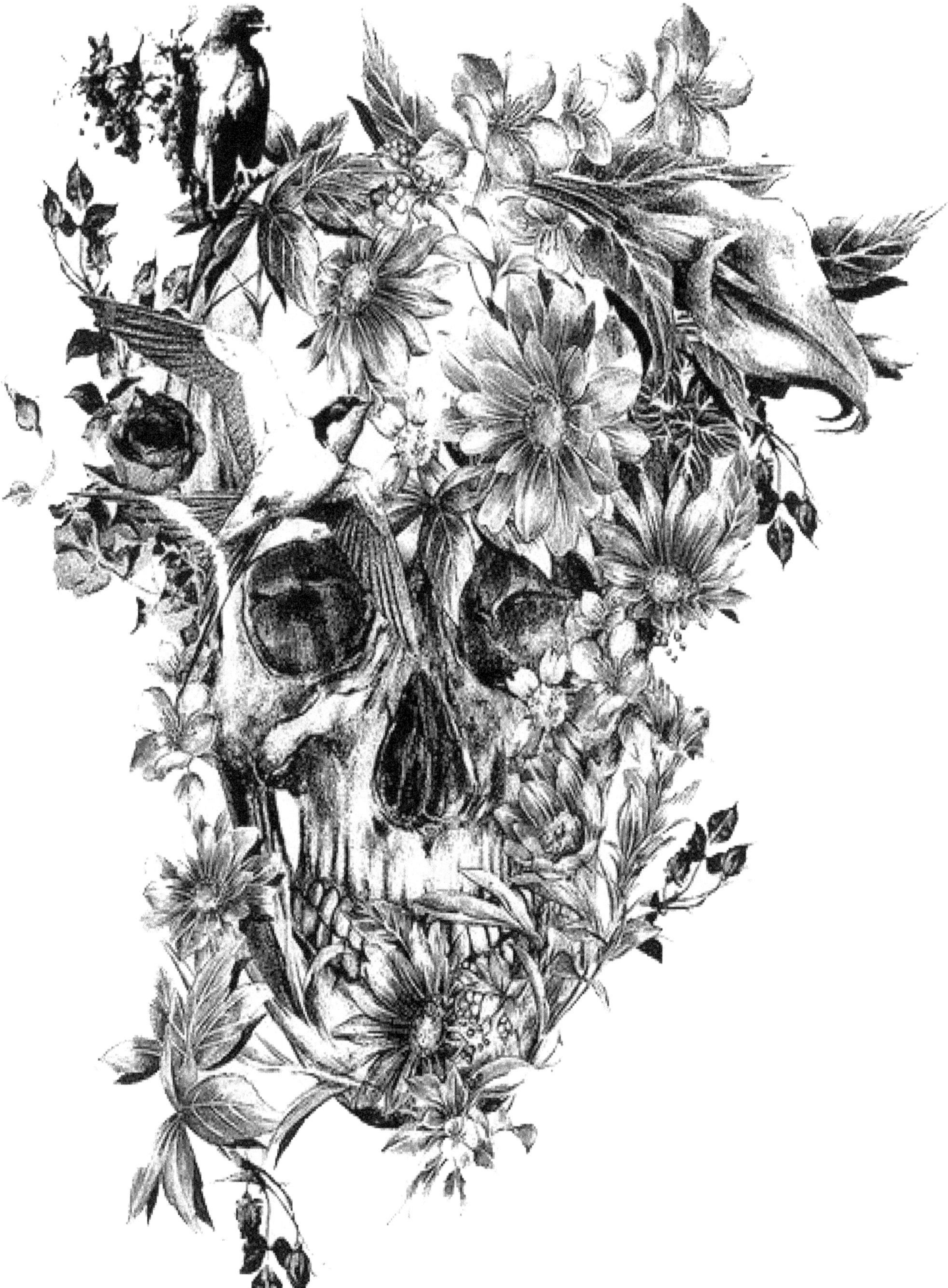

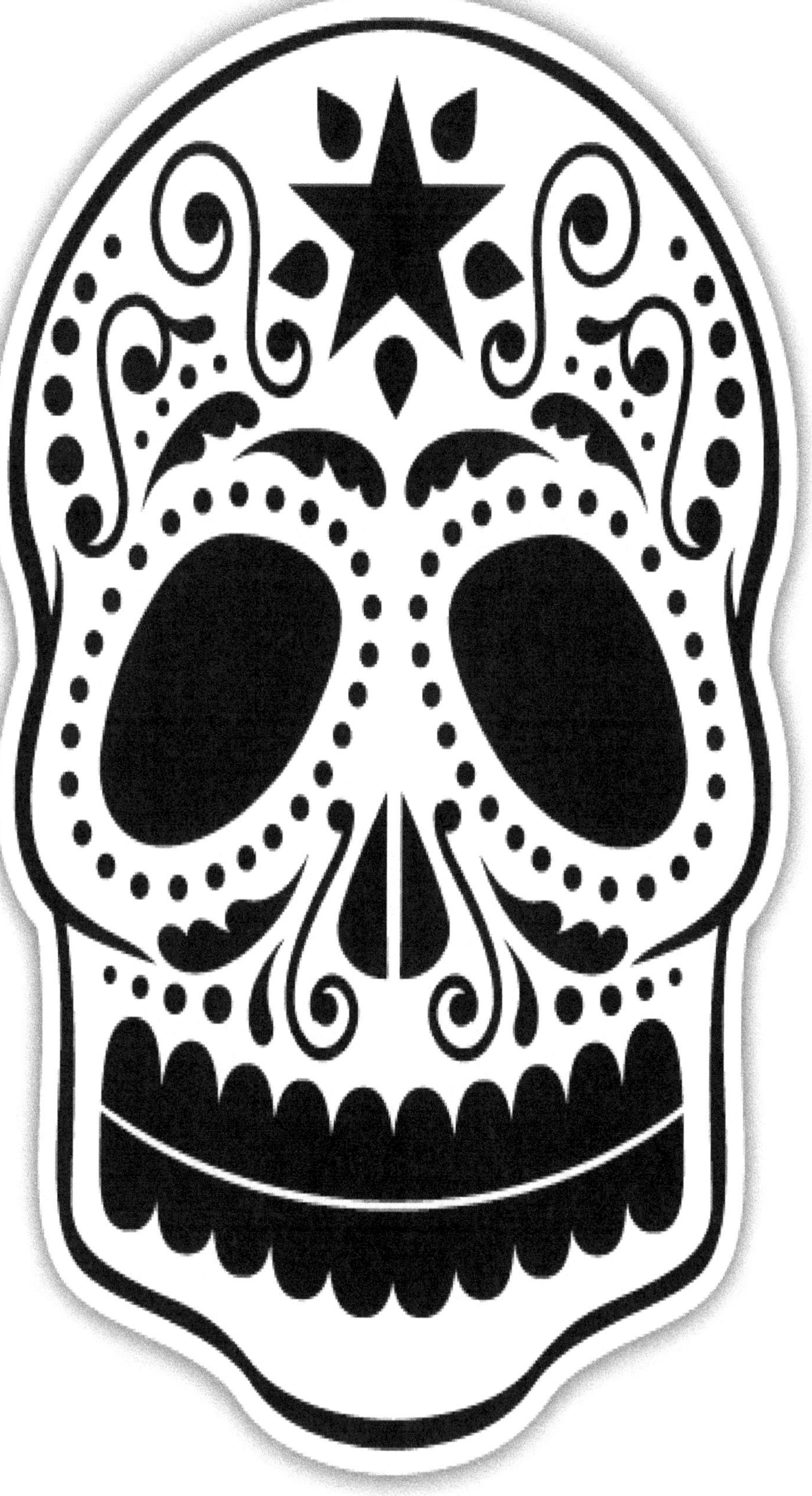

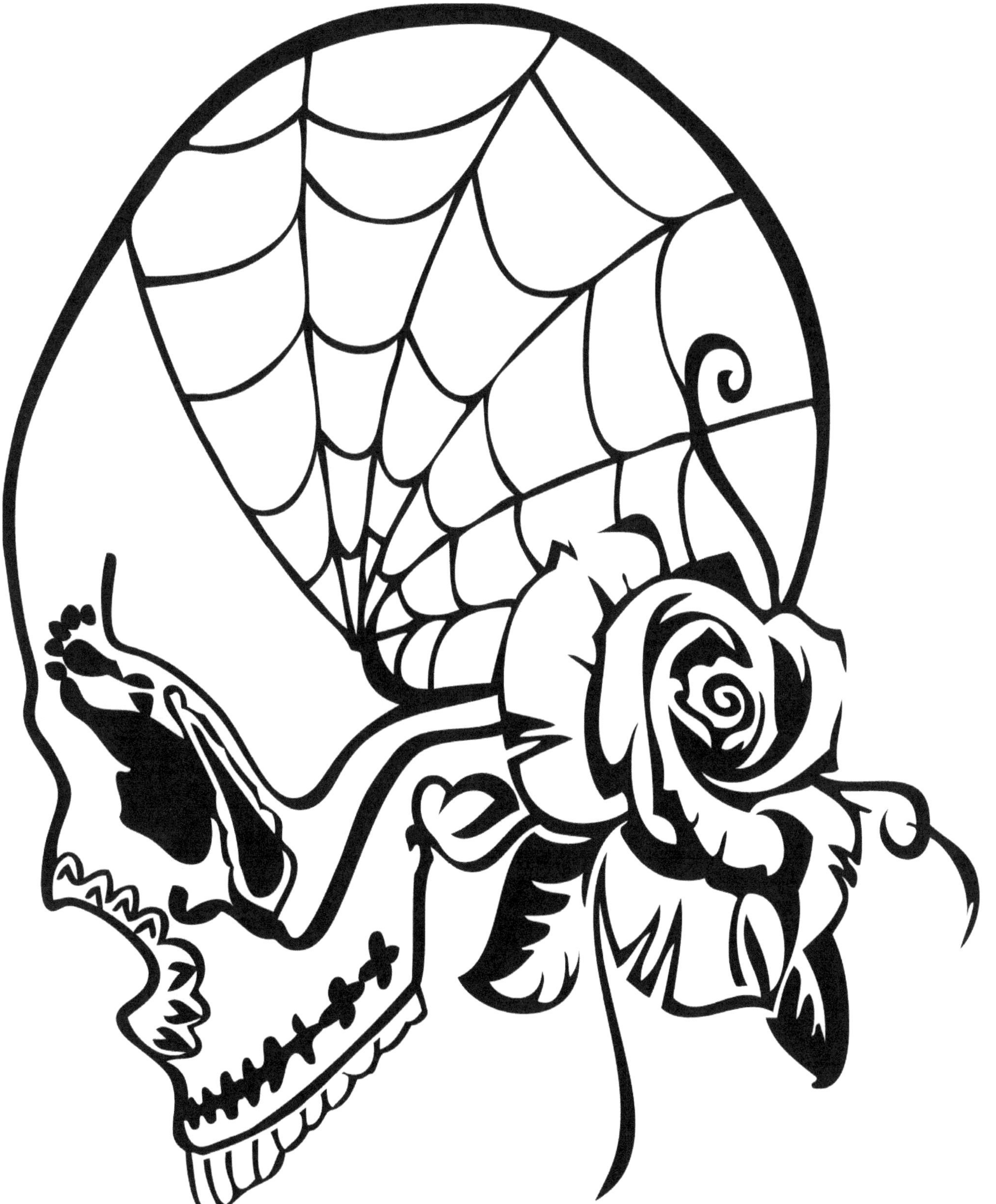

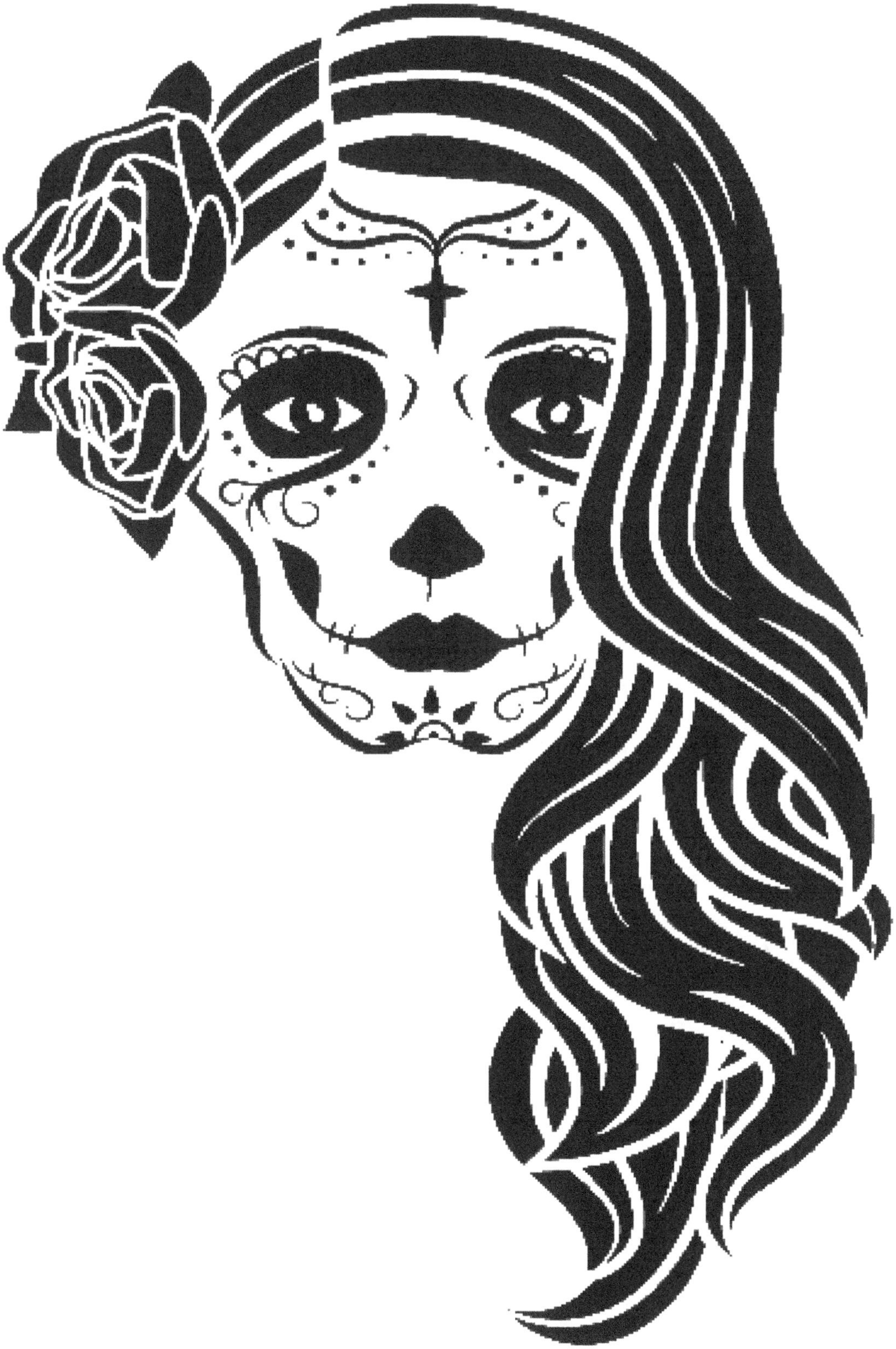

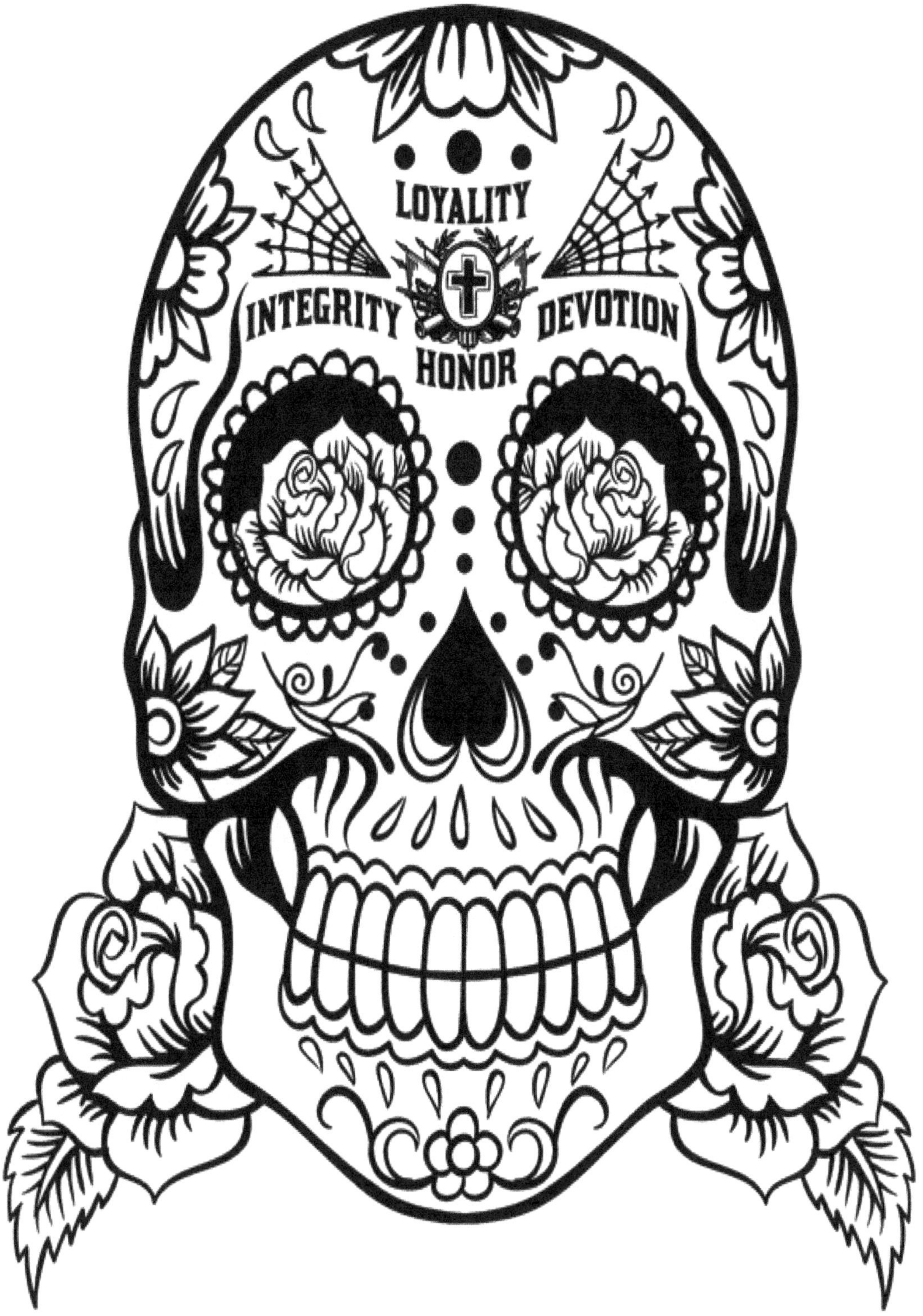
LOYALITY
INTEGRITY
DEVOTION
HONOR

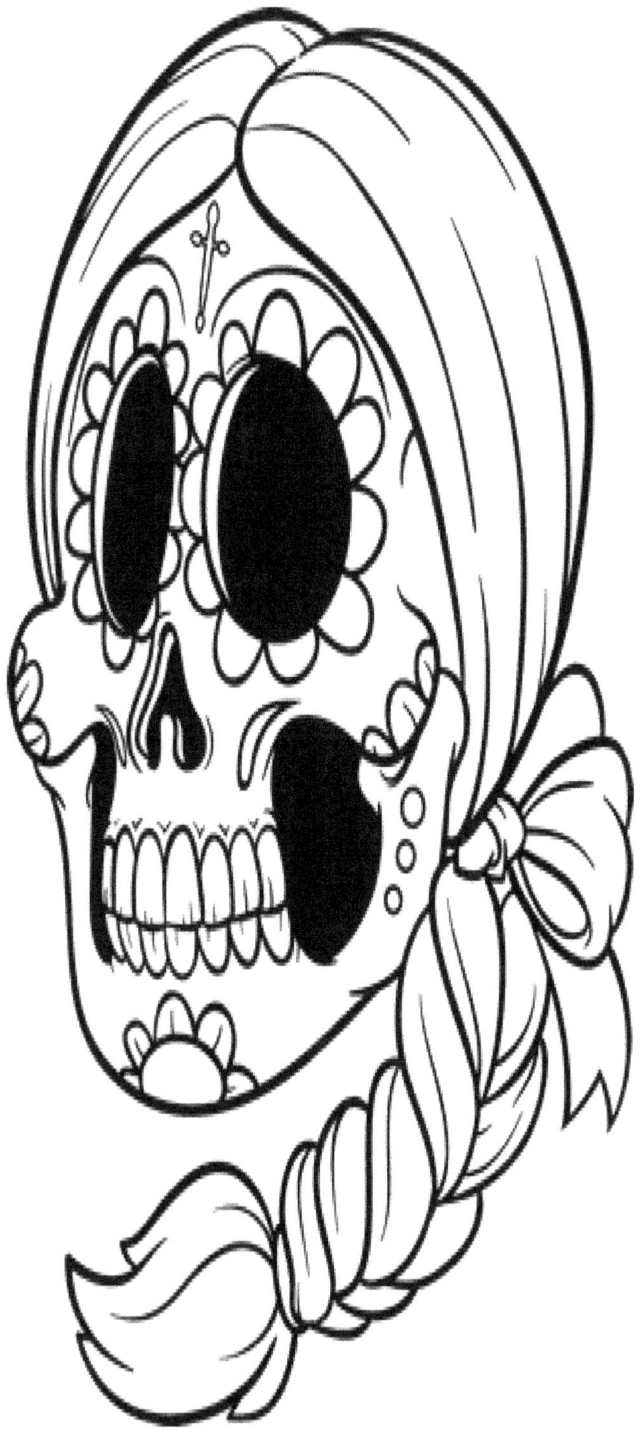

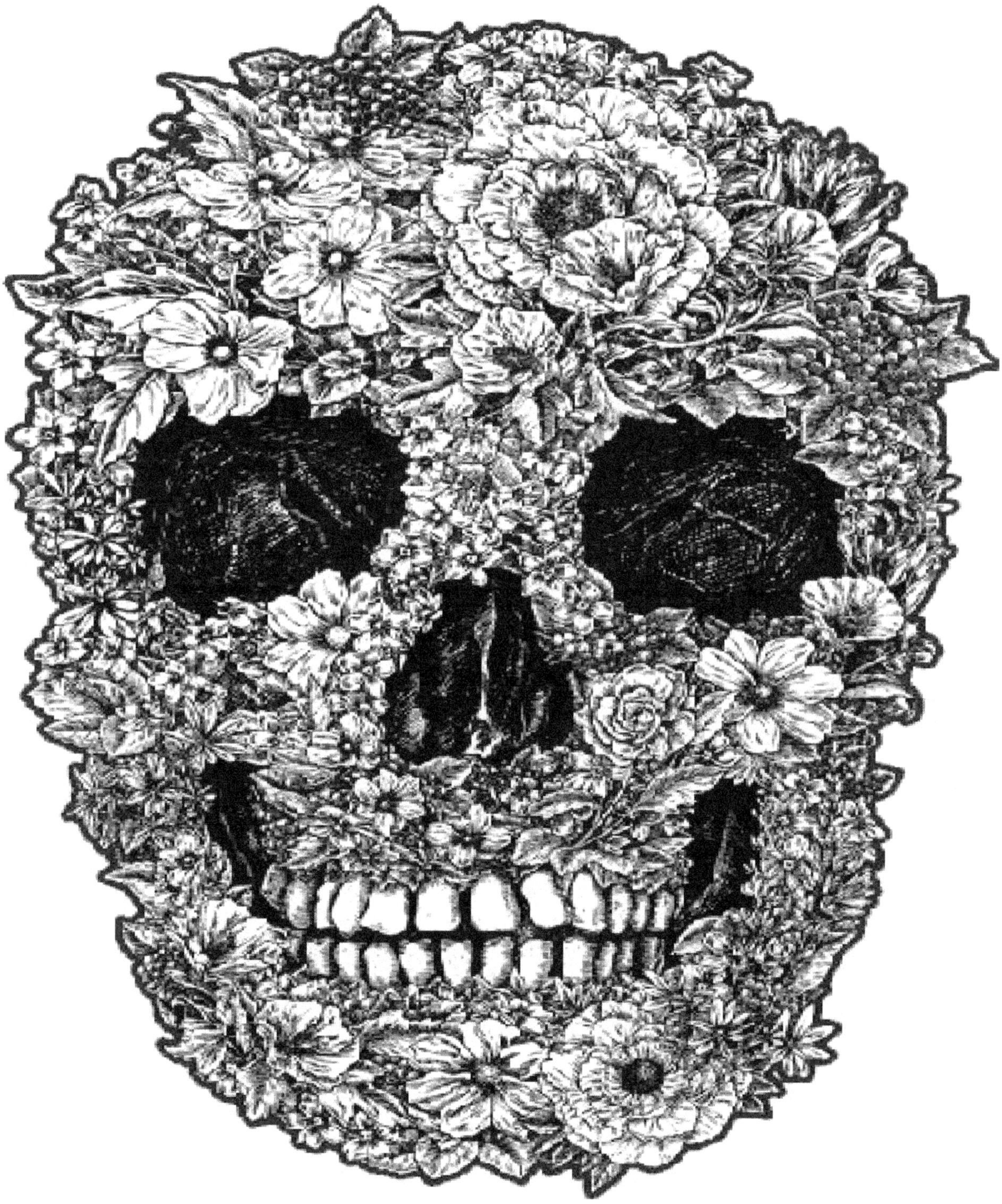